Dear _____

With love on your First Communion day

_____

_____

_____

From _____

Date _____

Translated from the original entitled
*Mein schönes Fest der Erstkommunion
Erinnerungsalbum*
© Verlag Herder Freiburg im Breisgau 2000
by Ulrike Graumann
Illustrations by Bernadette Nagel

English translation by *Anne Marie Swift*

© Pauline Books & Media, 2002
Middle Green
Slough SL3 6BS
England
www.pauline-uk.org e-mail: productions@pauline-uk.org

Printed by
SIG — Sociedade Gráfica, Lda. — Camarate (Portugal)
Printed March 2002
First reprinted June 2002
Second reprint February 2006
by AGAM, Cuneo, Italy

ISBN 0 953854019

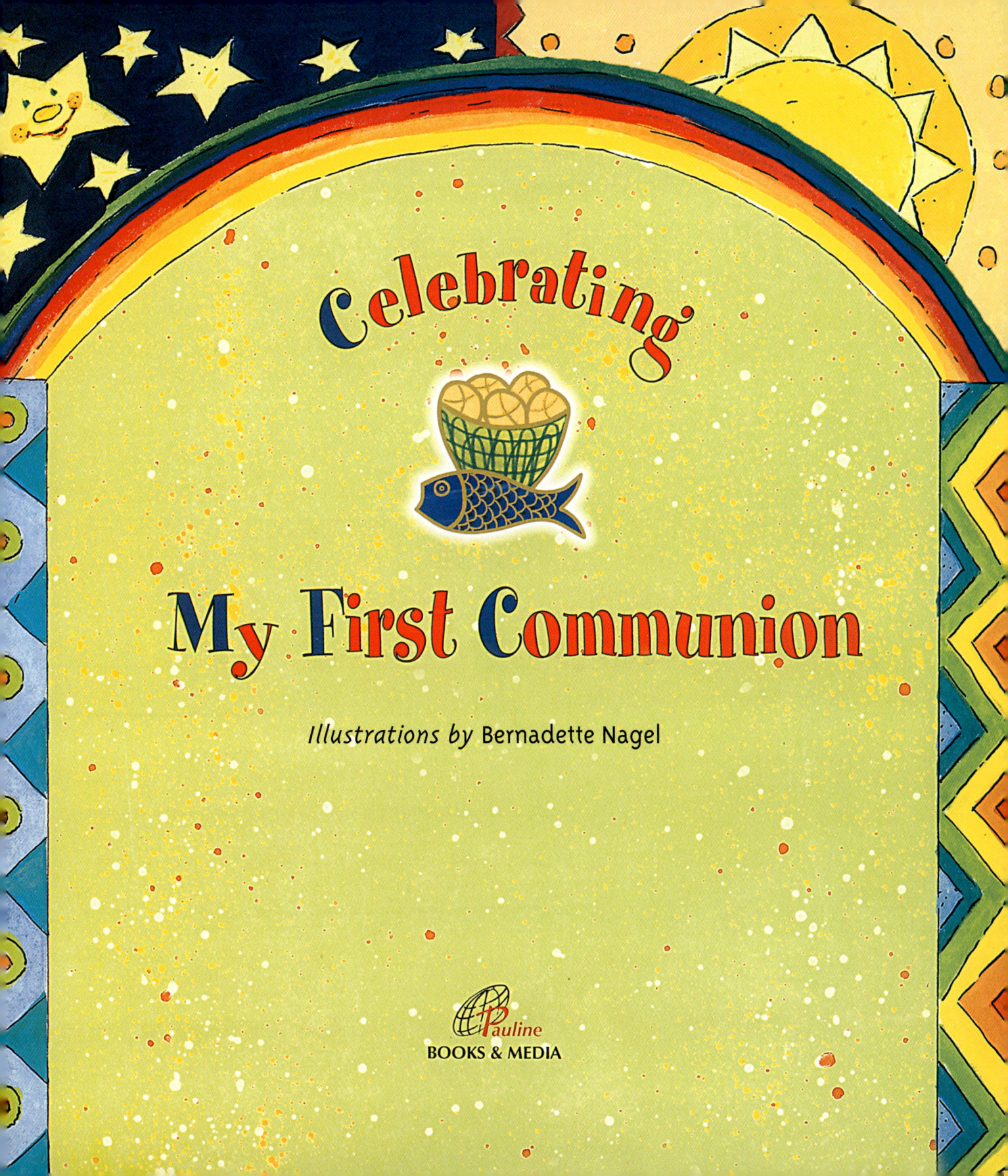

Celebrating
My First Communion

Illustrations by Bernadette Nagel

Pauline
BOOKS & MEDIA

This is a picture of me:

My name is _____

I am _____ years old.

I go to school at _____

I live at _____

In _____

These are the members of my family

_____

_____

_____

Our pets

This is a picture of my family:
(Draw a picture or stick in a photograph of your family)

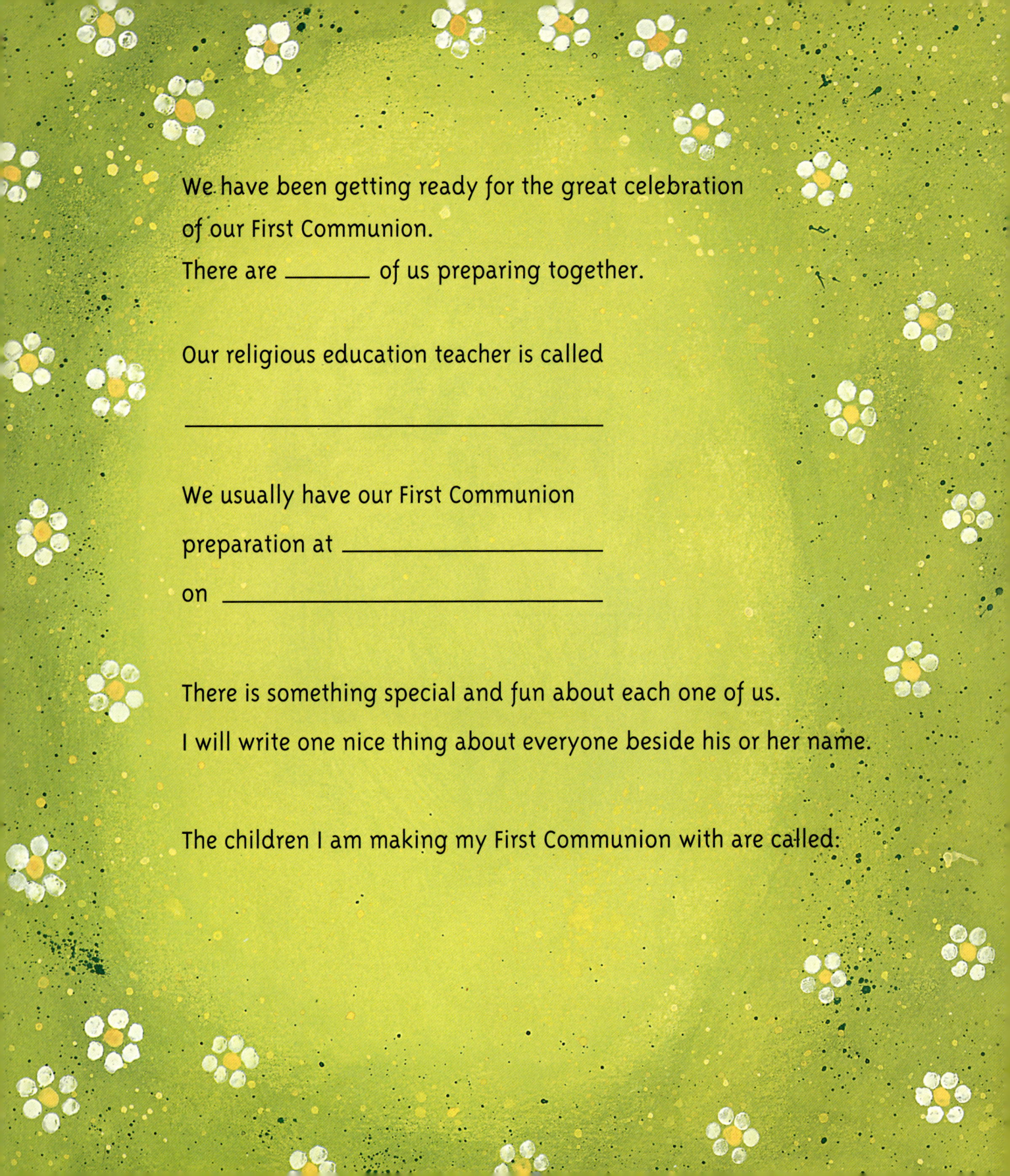

We have been getting ready for the great celebration of our First Communion.

There are _____ of us preparing together.

Our religious education teacher is called

_____

We usually have our First Communion preparation at _____

on _____

There is something special and fun about each one of us.
I will write one nice thing about everyone beside his or her name.

The children I am making my First Communion with are called:

Write the names of each of your friends on these petals. Or you might prefer to stick photos on or draw in their faces.

If you run out of petals, cut some more out of card or paper and add them to this page.

In our First Communion preparation we spoke about
_____
_____
_____
_____

We've done lots of great things.
We've met some great people.
We've been to some great places.
I'll write here what I liked best.

*I have some mementos of these happy times,
which I will stick on this page
(or draw some pictures to show them).*

Our parish is called

_____

It is in _____

Our parish priest is called

_____

This is what our church looks like.
Draw your church or stick in a photo.

My school is called

_____

It is in

Our religious education teacher whose name is

helped us get ready for our First Communion too.

*We read lots of wonderful things in the Bible.
Have a look at some of them again
in your religious education notebook.*

This is my favourite story:

The rainbow is an ancient symbol
of God's love for his people.
During the preparation for our First Communion
we learnt to recognise lots of symbols.

*Draw or cut out from a piece of paper or card
one of the symbols that you like the most,
and write out what it means.*

My personal rainbow with God,
I mean, my friendship with him,
began a few years ago
with two other signs (which are sacraments) of his love.

When I was little I received BAPTISM

on _____

in the parish of _____

I have also been to my FIRST CONFESSION

on _____

in the parish of _____

Now my friendship with Jesus is becoming stronger, it is growing like me.
I am now taking the third big step towards Jesus.
I receive the third sign of his love:
THE EUCHARIST, in my First Communion.

Today, _____
the _____
is a really special day.
We are celebrating
our First Communion!
There are _____ of us
making our First Communion.
Today Jesus welcomes us
to his table to share
his body and blood with us,
in the Mass.

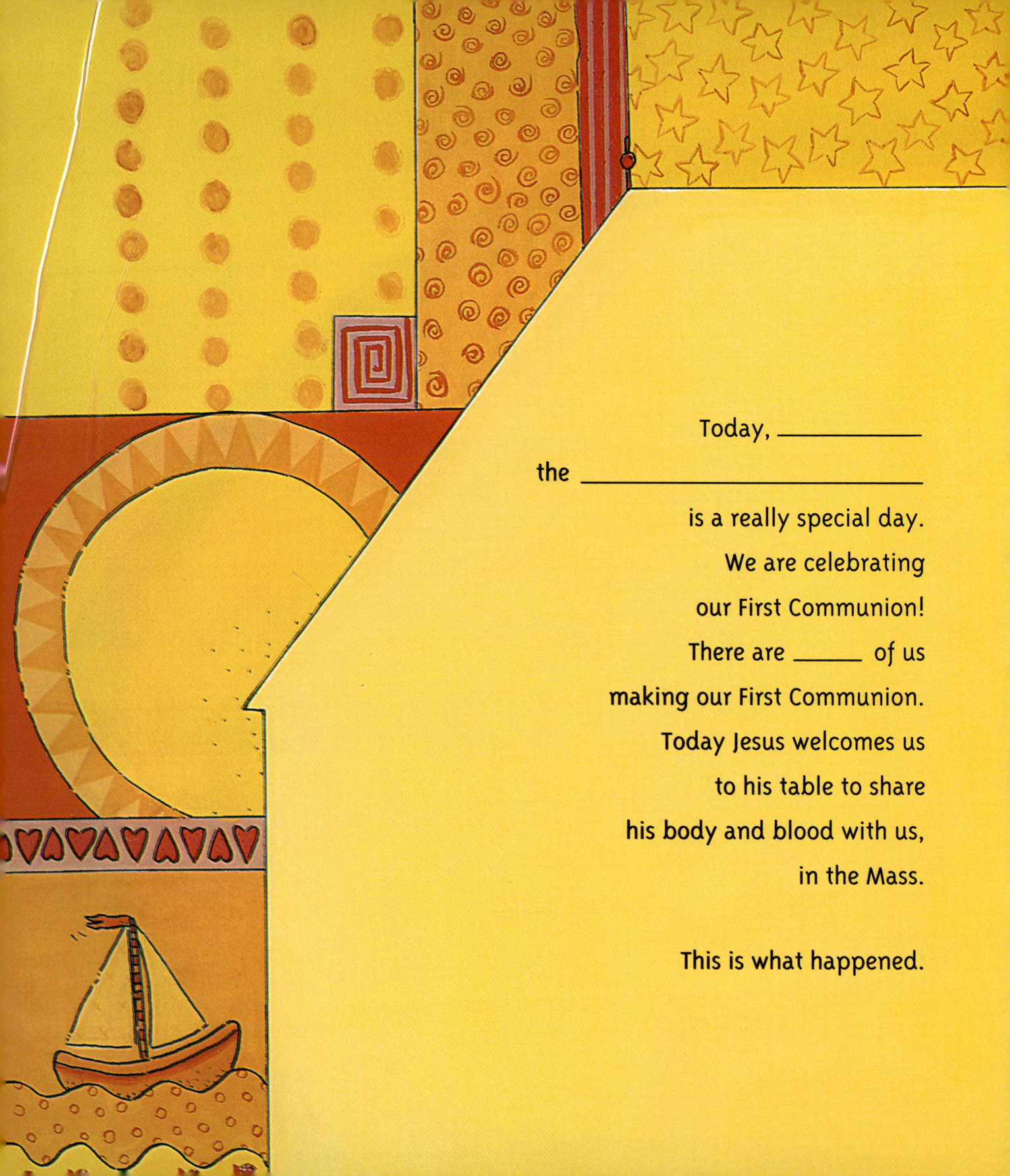

This is what happened.

We make our ENTRANCE into the church
in a procession with the priest and catechists,
while everyone is singing.
Like us, the church is prepared for a celebration.
There are flowers, candles, and special songs.
I feel   joyful ☐   nervous ☐   excited ☐

Then the priest WELCOMES us all
and presents us by name to the parish community.
The names of my companions are:

_____

_____

_____

_____

Together we say the "I CONFESS"
to ask forgiveness for all our mistakes.
For example, perhaps today I might let myself get distracted
by all the excitement, the new clothes, the photos and presents.
Help me, Lord, to concentrate on what is truly important:
my personal meeting with you in the Eucharist.

Then we say the GLORIA to praise the Lord
because he loves us and wants what is best for us and forgives us.

Together we listen attentively to the WORD OF GOD.
Today, as every day, God our good and loving father
wants to talk to us with his words.
The readings are:

_____

_____

_____

_____

Now the priest proclaims the Gospel.
It is great to hear what Jesus said and did.
We get ready to listen to the Gospel by singing the ALLELUIA
and by making a tiny sign of the cross with our thumb three times:
once on our forehead, so that the word of God might penetrate our minds,
once on our mouth, so that our words and actions
might testify to the word of God,
and once on our heart, so that the word of God may enter deeply within us.
This is what we desire especially today.
The Gospel reading is:

_____

_____

In his HOMILY, the priest talks to everyone
about the importance of the Eucharist and the joy it brings.
I really liked it when he said:

_____

_____

_____

_____

Then all together we recall our Baptism
by saying out loud the CREED, when we say that
we believe in God as our good and loving father, in Jesus our friend
and in the Holy Spirit who gives us the strength to love.
Or we repeat for ourselves the promises our parents and god-parents
made for us on the day of our Baptism.

We then pray the PRAYERS OF THE FAITHFUL.

We read some of these prayers out loud ourselves:

_____

_____

_____

_____

_____

At the OFFERTORY, we bring up to the altar the bread and wine, which will soon be transformed into the body and blood of Jesus Christ. We also bring to Jesus other gifts (e.g. candles, the Bible, catechism book, drawings...) with these words:

_____
_____
_____
_____
_____

The priest blesses the bread and wine saying:

"**Blessed are you, Lord, God of all creation.**
Through your goodness we have this bread to offer,
which earth has given and human hands have made.
It will become for us the bread of life".
And we reply: "**Blessed be God for ever**".

"**Blessed are you, Lord, God of all creation.**
Through your goodness we have this wine to offer,
fruit of the vine and work of human hands.
It will become our spiritual drink".
And we reply: "**Blessed be God for ever**".

The priest says
the EUCHARISTIC PRAYER.
This is the prayer to thank God
for all his gifts,
especially for Jesus his Son,
who loves us and gave his life for us.
It goes something like this:
"God, our Father
You have brought us here together
so that we can give you thanks and praise
for all the wonderful things you have done.
We thank you for all that is beautiful in the world
and for the happiness you have given us.
We praise you for daylight
and for your word which lights up our minds.
We praise you for the earth, and all the people who live on it
and for our life which comes from you.
We know that you are good.
You love us and do great things for us".

So all together in joyful voice we sing.

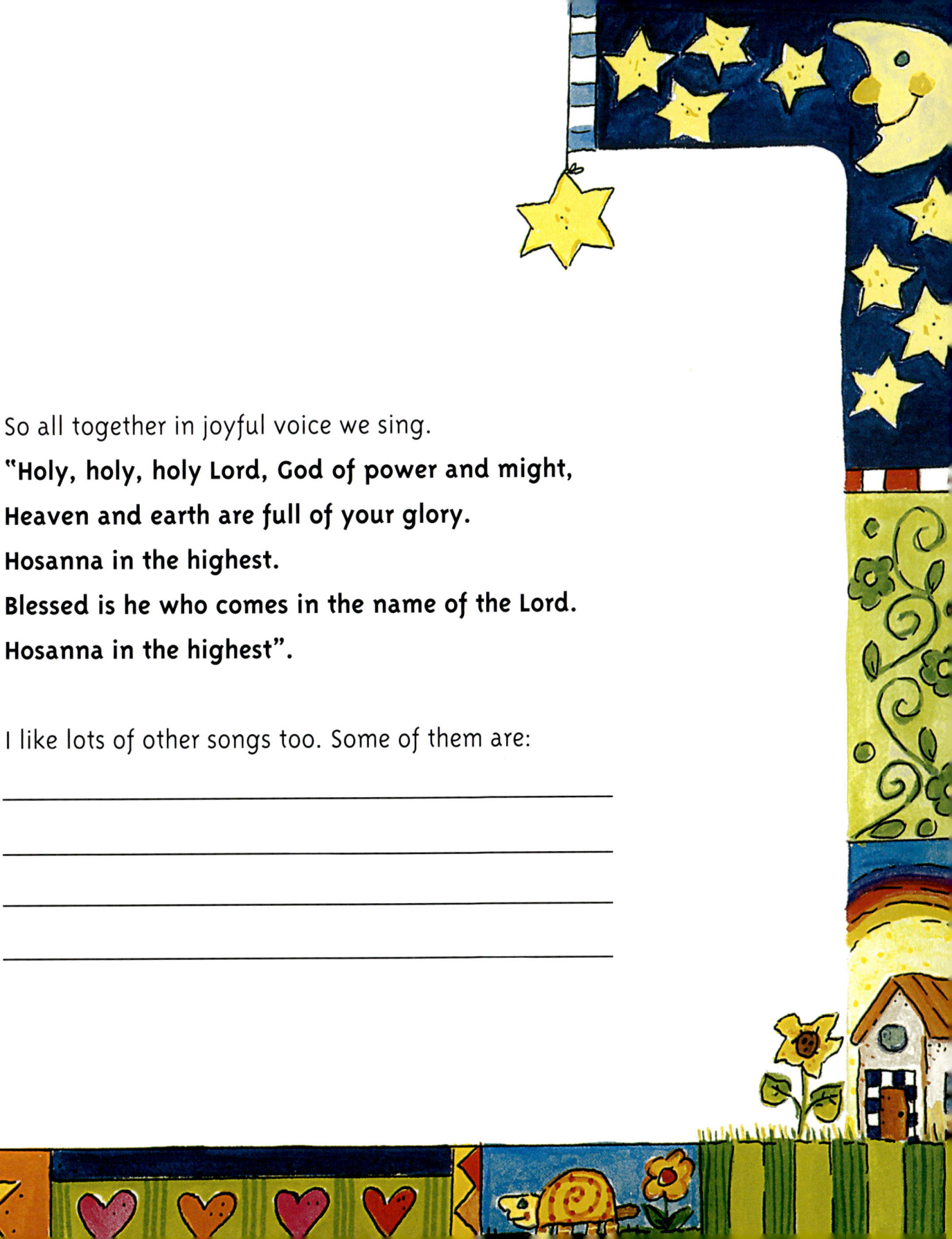

"Holy, holy, holy Lord, God of power and might,
Heaven and earth are full of your glory.
Hosanna in the highest.
Blessed is he who comes in the name of the Lord.
Hosanna in the highest".

I like lots of other songs too. Some of them are:

_____

_____

_____

_____

It is now the most important and solemn moment of the Mass,
the CONSECRATION of the bread and wine.
My friends and I really pay attention as
the priest repeats the words and actions of Jesus at the Last Supper.

"The night before he died,
Jesus your Son showed us how much you love us.
When he was at supper with his disciples, he took bread
and gave you thanks and praise.
Then he broke the bread, gave it to his friends and said:
'Take this, all of you, and eat it:
This is my body which will be given up for you'.

When supper was ended,
Jesus took the cup that was filled with wine.
He thanked you, gave it to his friends and said:
'Take this, all of you, and drink from it:
This is the cup of my blood, the blood of the new and everlasting covenant.
It will be shed for you and for all so that sins may be forgiven'.
Then he said to them: 'Do this in memory of me'".

The bread and wine are now the body and blood of Christ.

The OUR FATHER prayer is wonderful:

we say it all together, sometimes we can hold hands, to remind us that

God truly is the father of everyone.

He is a good, tender, caring father, who wants all his children to be happy.

I like this phrase of the "Our Father" best

_____

because _____

At the SIGN OF PEACE, we greet each other,

happy to be sharing our First Communion day.

We know that Jesus wants us to be united

with one another in order to be united with him.

He told us: "Love one another as I have loved you.

By this they will know that you are my disciples".

On this solemn occasion, I promise in a special way to live for peace.

I will try to bring peace

in my family ☐   at school ☐   with my friends ☐

with people I find it difficult to like ☐

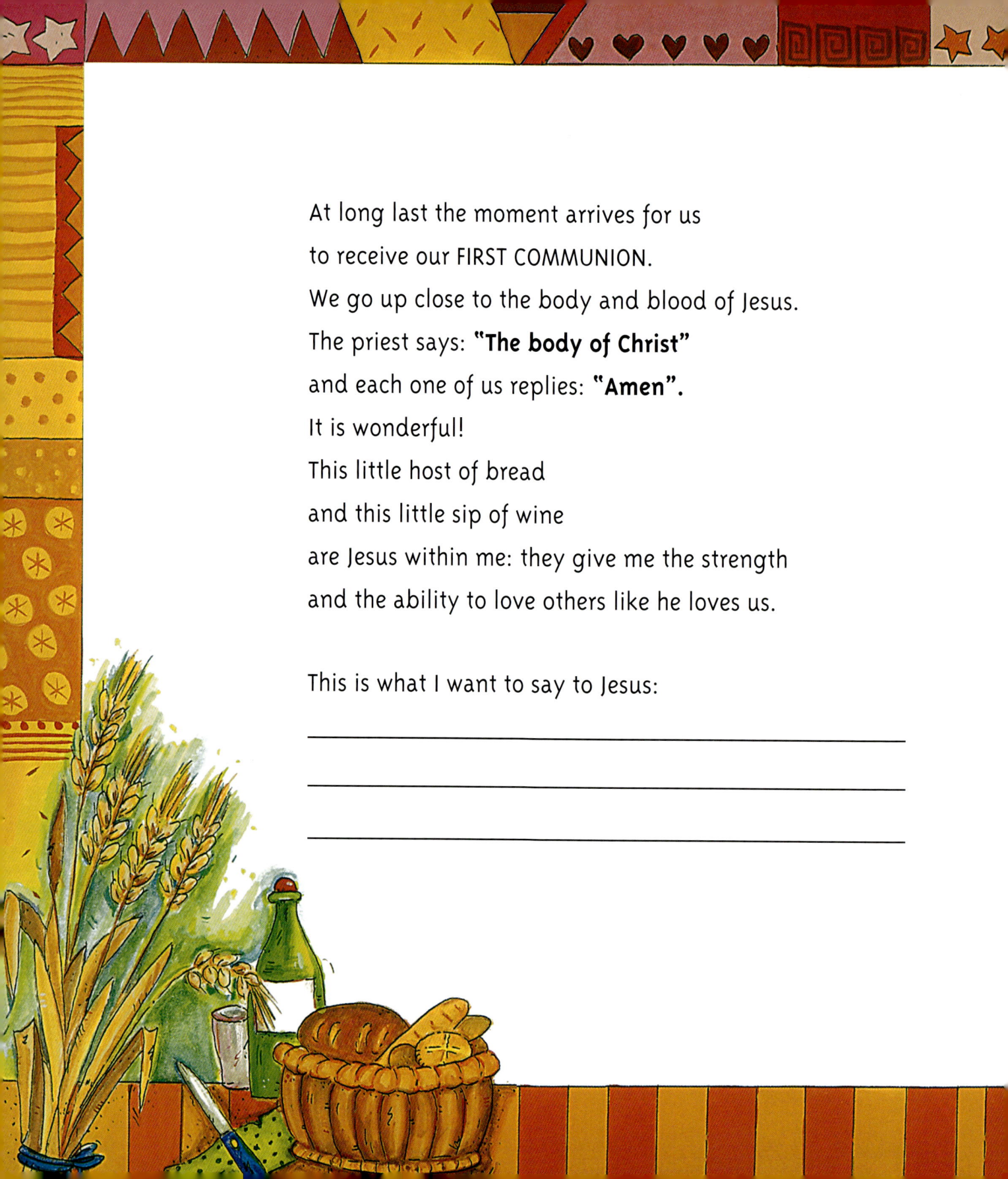

At long last the moment arrives for us
to receive our FIRST COMMUNION.
We go up close to the body and blood of Jesus.
The priest says: **"The body of Christ"**
and each one of us replies: **"Amen"**.
It is wonderful!
This little host of bread
and this little sip of wine
are Jesus within me: they give me the strength
and the ability to love others like he loves us.

This is what I want to say to Jesus:

_____

_____

_____

At the end of Mass
the priest gives us all a BLESSING like this one:
"The Lord be with you.
May God the Father, Son and Holy Spirit
bless you and be with you always.
Go in peace to love and serve the Lord".

Jesus is with me, everywhere I am, all the time,
so I can be very happy and truly go in peace
living in his love every day of my life.
Now the greatest adventure of all has begun:
being a true friend of Jesus.

Here are some photographs of my First Communion day.

*Here I am with my friends,
my catechist or teacher and our priest.*

Lots of people are celebrating
my First Communion with me.
They have sent me their good wishes
and promised their prayers.
I don't want to forget them ever.
So some of them have signed this page for me.

These are some of the most special cards
I received for my First Communion.

My First Communion day
is an extra-special day!

(This page is for writing down some of the highlights)

Some more of my favourite photographs or cards.

This is a special diary page of my album,
to write my feelings, impressions
and happiest memories
of my First Communion day.

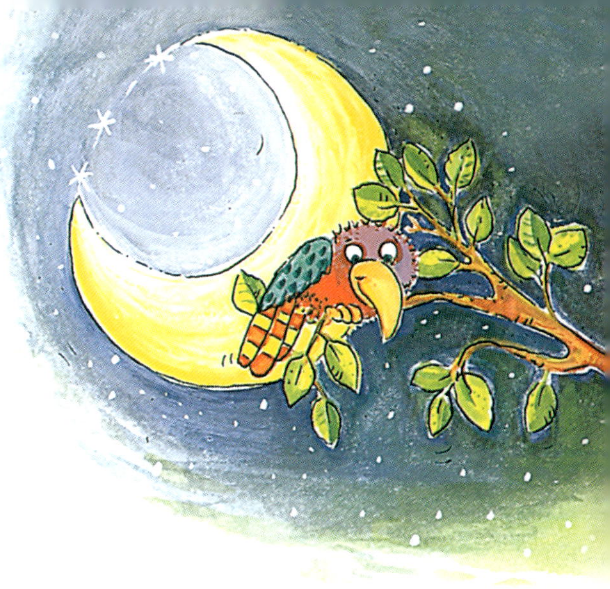

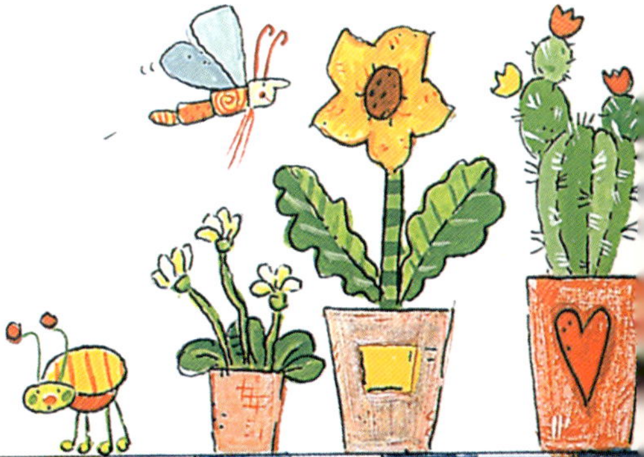

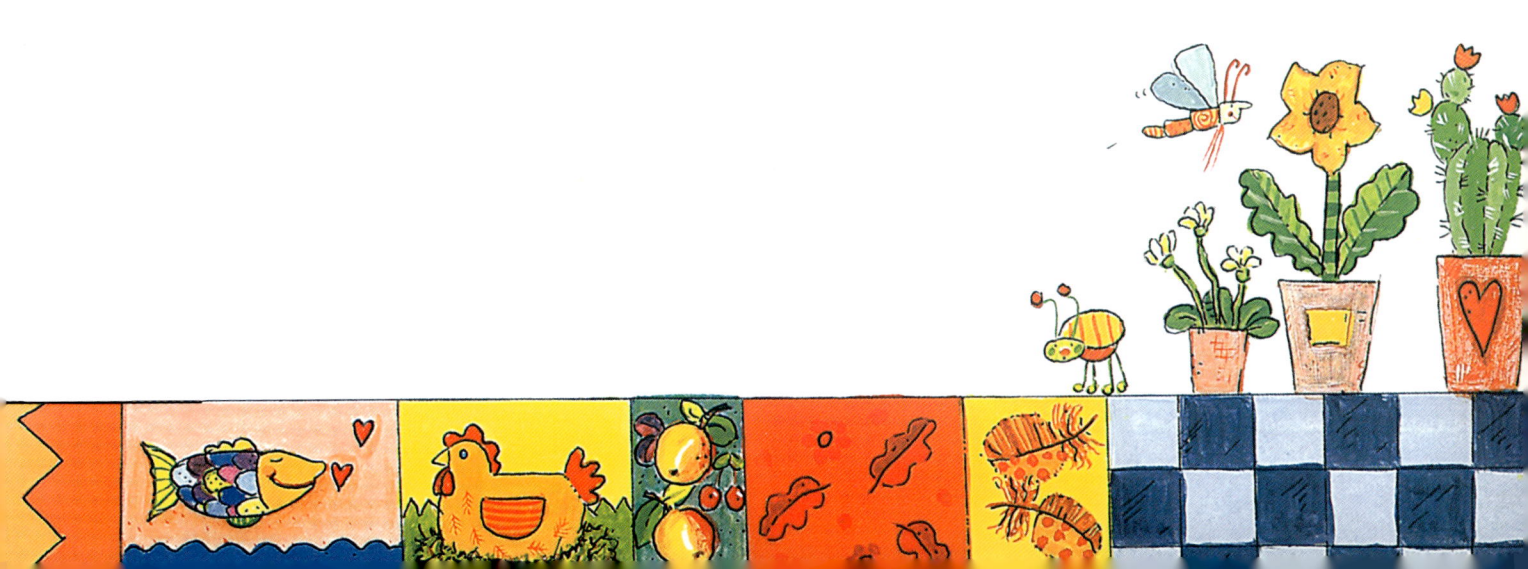

Together with my First Communion friends, I have decided to belong to Jesus. Together we can make a difference to our world. Here is a little story about this.

THE LITTLE KINDNESS

Once upon a time there was a little kindness. Yes, really! a little kindness. He was so little that most people ignored him most of the time. Nobody seemed to notice him, and he often nearly got trampled under people's feet, or bicycle wheels or cars.

"Life near people who are always in a rush can prove dangerous!" the little kindness thought to himself. "When everything's ok, they ignore me, and when things are going badly, they walk all over me. Well, I've had enough. I'm leaving. I'm going to find my own way in the world".

So off he went through the countryside and from town to town. He would say to the people he met along the way: "Isn't it great to meet you here. I'm a little kindness. By any chance, do you happen to need me?" But no-one paid any attention. Except one man, who replied: "What use is a little kindness to me? I have a great destiny ahead of me!" and he rushed off.

The little kindness became sadder and sadder. One day he arrived in the land of darkness, where the sun never shines and the stars never come out. There was no light and the people were sad and miserable. The little kindness saw a tired old man who lived all alone.

"Isn't it great to meet you here. I am a little kindness. Can I help you in any way?"

"Get out of here!" shouted the old man. "How could you help me? The world is dark and life is hard. What difference can a little kindness make? None at all!" And with that, he went inside and slammed the door, like his heart, shut fast so no light and no friendship could enter.

The little kindness went away sad.

He walked on and on until he came to the sea.

"I can't go on any more", he sighed. "I am too small for this great big world". And he cried and cried all through the cold dark night.

After shedding many bitter tears, suddenly he began to notice a warm feeling inside. Slowly, he opened his eyes and saw a thin ray of sunlight gently caressing him.

"Wow, you're beautiful!" murmured the little kindness.

"Do you think so?" shimmered the little ray of sunshine, becoming a touch brighter.

"Who are you and where do you come from?" asked the little kindness.

"I'm a ray of the sun. I caress the darknesss and bring in the new day".

"All on your own?" replied the little kindness rather doubtfully. "You know that people don't take any notice of little things like you and me".

"But I have many friends" said the ray of sunshine and she turned round. "Look, they're on their way. May I introduce them to you?

This is my friend called 'thank you'.

And here is 'the little helping hand' and there's 'the friendly smile'.

'Good morning' and his cousin 'the goodnight kiss' are both good friends of mine.

I've not finished yet. Here is 'a little bit of time', and this is 'the tender cuddle', while over there 'the big hug' is just arriving. And..."

"Hold on, hold on!" cried the little kindness. "I'll never remember all their names!"

"That doesn't matter", said the ray of sunshine, looking thoughtfully at the little kindness. "I think you'll fit in well with the rest of us. Would you like to join us as we travel round the world?"

"You bet!" shouted the little kindness excitedly. "I think life will be great fun with all of you. Yes, let's go and shift the darkness".

So they set off together. And wherever they go they awaken joy in people's hearts, freeing them from the deepest darkness, just like that!

Now wouldn't you like to join them too?

ALBERT ALTENNÄHR

The little kindness and all his friends are waiting for you.
You too can help make a difference to the world.

Dear God

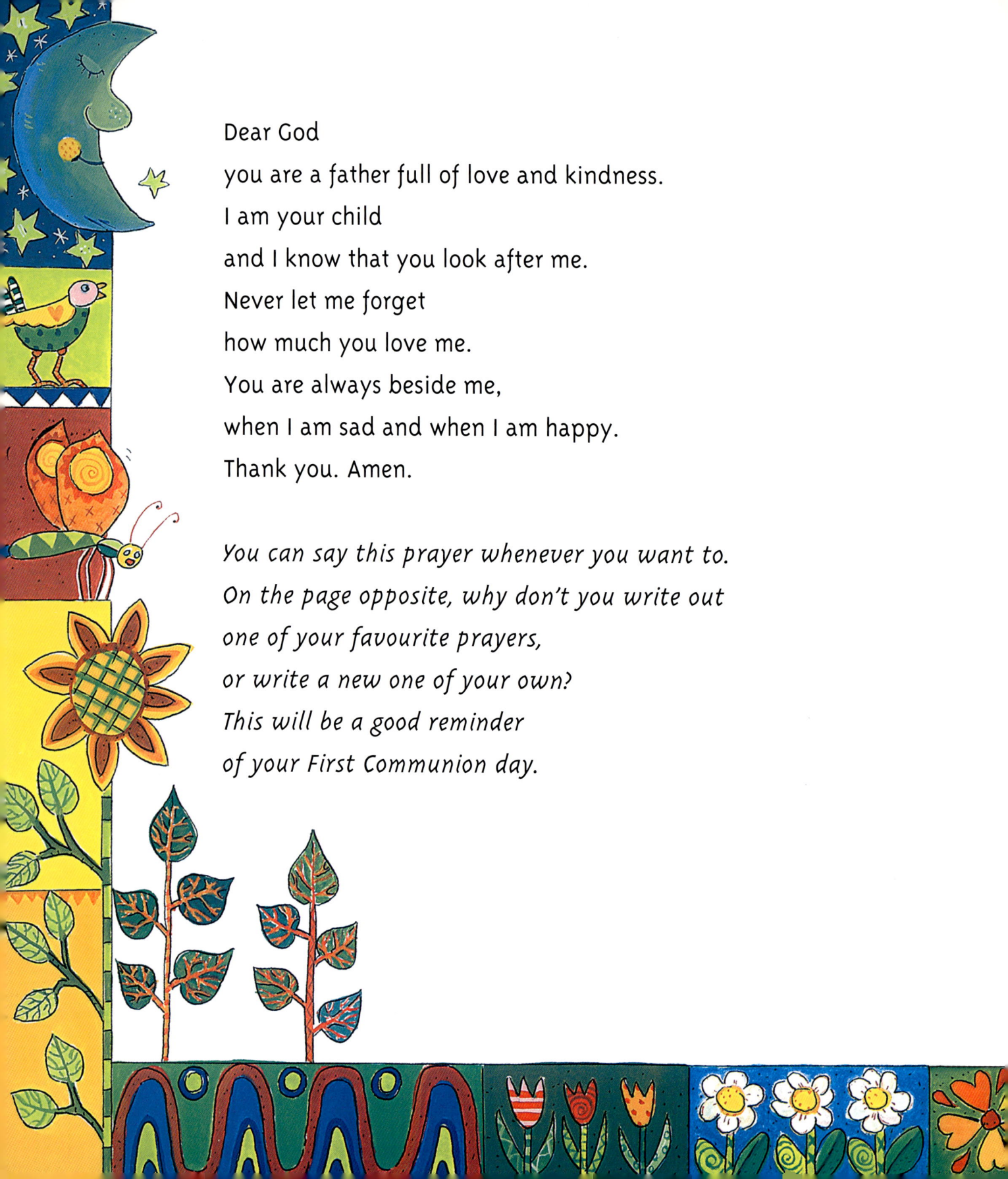

you are a father full of love and kindness.

I am your child

and I know that you look after me.

Never let me forget

how much you love me.

You are always beside me,

when I am sad and when I am happy.

Thank you. Amen.

You can say this prayer whenever you want to.
On the page opposite, why don't you write out
one of your favourite prayers,
or write a new one of your own?
This will be a good reminder
of your First Communion day.

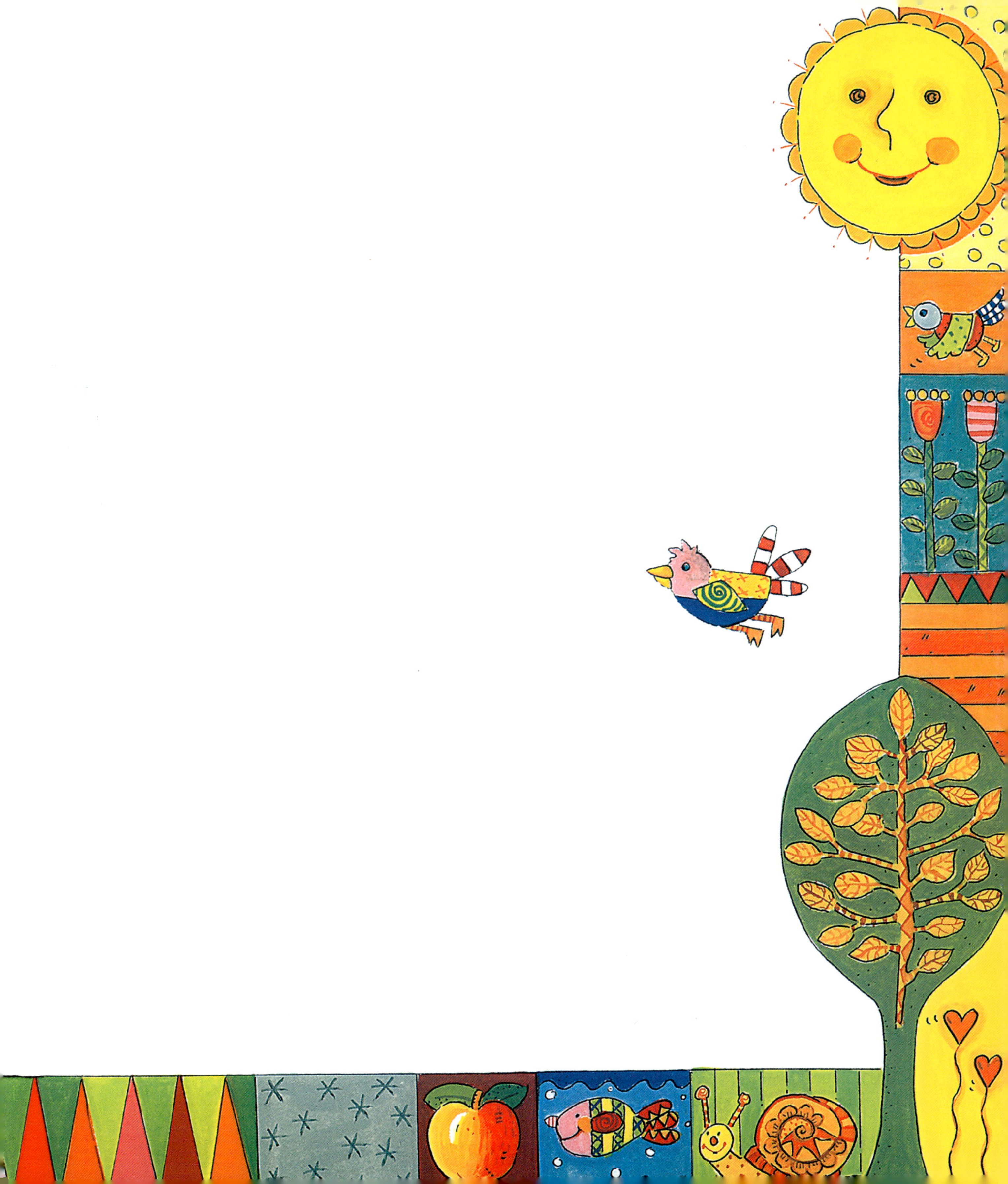

Here are three ideas for making thank you cards to send to all the people who helped to make your First Communion such a special day.

THANK YOU

Cut the shape of waves out of blue-coloured paper (different shades) and stick them onto a piece of card. Cut out the shape of a fish from another small piece of card, or even from a piece of material. Then stick it on top of the waves.

Fold a piece of card in half.
On the top part
cut out the shape of a heart.
On the inside stick one
of your photos or another picture,
so you can see it
through the heart shape.

On a piece of coloured card
stick a strip
of different coloured card
(this example is green).
Stick on dried flowers
tied with some
coloured ribbon.